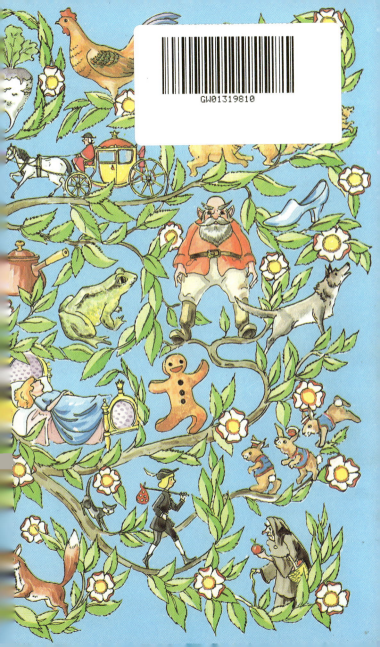

To read fluently is one of the basic aims of anyone learning English as a foreign language. **And it's never too early to start.** Ladybird Graded Readers are interesting but simple stories designed to encourage children between the ages of 6 and 12 to read with pleasure.

Reading is an excellent way of reinforcing language already acquired, as well as broadening a child's vocabulary. Ladybird Graded Readers use a limited number of grammatical structures and a carefully controlled vocabulary, but where the story demands it, a small number of words outside the basic vocabulary are introduced. In ***The Sorcerer's Apprentice*** the following words are outside the basic vocabulary for this grade:

apprentice, axe, broom, castle, cauldron, chop, crops, eagle, flash of lightning, grape, hall, harvest, raven, sorcerer, spell, tail, wand, wine, wing

Further details of the structures and vocabulary used at each grade can be found in the Ladybird Graded Readers *leaflet.*

British Library Cataloguing in Publication Data
Ullstein, Sue
  The Sorcerer's apprentice.
  1. English language—Readers
  I. Title II. McKie, Ken
  428.6
  ISBN 0-7214-1351-X

First edition

Published by Ladybird Books Ltd Loughborough Leicestershire UK
Ladybird Books Inc Auburn Maine 04210 USA

© LADYBIRD BOOKS LTD MCMXC
All rights reserved. No part of this publication may be reproduced, stored in a retrieval system, or transmitted in any form or by any means, electronic, mechanical, photo-copying, recording or otherwise, without the prior consent of the copyright owner.

Printed in England

The Sorcerer's Apprentice

retold by Sue Ullstein
illustrated by Ken McKie

Ladybird Books

Our story begins a long time ago in a little village in a valley at the foot of a mountain. The mountain is very high and clouds often cover it. At the top of the mountain there is a great castle, but the people of the village have never climbed the mountain. No one from the valley has ever been inside the castle.

Life in the valley is good. The people work hard, but they are happy.

No one is ever hungry. They grow good crops: corn for bread, grapes for wine, apples, pears and vegetables. Every autumn the harvest is good. There is always enough food for everyone in the village.

Then one autumn a strange thing happens. The people go out into the fields to bring in the harvest but there is no harvest! All their crops have disappeared. There is no corn. There are no apples, no pears, no grapes, no vegetables.

"Where have our crops gone?" an angry farmer shouts.

"Who has stolen our corn?" a woman cries.

"I'll catch the thieves!" another man shouts. "And I'll kill them!"

The people look for the thieves for a long time, but they do not catch them.

Soon winter comes. It is very cold. But the people of the village have kept food from other harvests so no one is too hungry.

In the spring the people plant their seeds again.

"The harvest will be good this autumn," they tell one another.

In the autumn, the men of the village stay in the fields every night. They want to stop the thieves. They do not want to lose this year's harvest, too.

But early one morning an old woman goes out into the fields. Soon she runs back to the village.

"Help! Help!" she cries. "Someone has stolen our crops again. There's nothing in the fields!"

"But how?" one man asks. "Six men stayed in the fields as usual last night. Didn't they see anything?"

"No, they didn't," the old lady replies. "I think it's magic. We're going to be hungry this winter. What shall we do?"

A boy called Jim comes forward. "Let me help," he says. "I'm strong and clever. I'll catch the thieves."

Jim runs out of the village and up the mountain. He climbs quickly.

Soon he is up in the clouds. He cannot see very well but he is not afraid. He sings to himself happily.

"I'll soon be at the top of the mountain," he says.

"You're there already!" a deep voice says.

Jim is very surprised. An old man is standing in front of him. He is wearing very strange clothes. He has a magic wand in his left hand and a large black raven is sitting on his right arm.

"Who are you?" Jim asks.

"I'm the Sorcerer of this mountain," the old man says.

"It's late," the Sorcerer says to Jim. "My castle is very near. Come and stay the night with me."

Jim follows the Sorcerer. Inside the castle he sees great piles of food everywhere.

The raven flies down. "That's the harvest from your valley," he tells Jim. "The Sorcerer has stolen it for himself."

"I'll kill him for that!" Jim cries.

"How?" the raven asks. "He's a sorcerer. He can do magic. He'll kill you with one of his spells before you can kill him."

"But what shall I do?" Jim says. "He mustn't steal our harvest every year."

"Stay here and learn his secrets," the raven says. "Then you can use the spells against him!"

Suddenly the Sorcerer turns round.

"Do you want a job?" he asks Jim. "Because I need an apprentice."

"Yes, sir," Jim replies. "I'll do the job if you give me lessons in magic."

"Good," the Sorcerer answers. "Come with me. I'll show you the castle."

The castle is very, very big. The Sorcerer takes Jim from room to room. At last they come to the Great Hall.

"He does his magic here," Jim thinks.

There are big books everywhere in the Great Hall. They look very heavy. In the middle of the room there is a great black cauldron. Green smoke is coming out of it.

"You must fill that cauldron every

day," the Sorcerer tells Jim. "It must *never* be empty."

"Yes, sir. I understand," Jim answers. "I'll start work at once."

"When you finish your work, I'll teach you my magic," the Sorcerer says.

And so Jim becomes the Sorcerer's apprentice. He works hard from morning till night. But he never finishes all the work and so the Sorcerer never teaches him any magic.

Jim and the raven become good friends. The raven tells Jim about his life. "I've lived in this castle for a long

time," he says. "The Sorcerer put a spell on me and now I can't leave the castle. I can fly round the castle, but if I try to fly down into the valley, my wings don't work. Will you take me with you when you escape, Jim?"

"What do you mean, 'escape'?" Jim asks. "I'm not a prisoner here. I needn't escape. I can walk out of here now and go home." And he picks up the raven and walks out of the gate.

But suddenly he stops. He tries very hard but he cannot move forward.

"You see!" the raven says. "You're not free, either. We're the Sorcerer's prisoners."

"Oh, no," Jim says sadly. "The Sorcerer has put a spell on me, too. What shall I do?"

He thinks for a moment and then he

says, "I know, I must learn some magic quickly. Then I can stop his spells."

But every day the Sorcerer makes Jim work harder. There is never time for lessons in magic. And the Sorcerer never lets Jim hear his magic words when he makes his spells.

Jim hates bringing the water for the cauldron. The river is far away from the Great Hall and he has to walk there and back many times each day. The heavy buckets of water hurt his arms.

One day the raven says to Jim, "You must learn some of the Sorcerer's magic words soon. We can't stay here for ever. You must be cleverer. You've never heard any of his magic words yet, have you?"

"No, I haven't," Jim replies.

"I've tried to hear the words," Jim goes on, "but he says them very quietly."

So Jim and the raven try harder to hear the Sorcerer's magic words for his spells.

They hide behind the Sorcerer. They hide under his table. But the Sorcerer is clever, too. He never lets Jim hear his spells. And he makes Jim work more and more. Now Jim has to work at night, too.

One night Jim is very, very tired. He does not go to his room. He falls asleep in a dark corner near the Sorcerer's chair. The Sorcerer does not see him. He is too busy with his spells. Suddenly he drops a glass bottle. It falls off the table and onto the floor. It breaks into a thousand pieces.

The noise wakes Jim. He looks at the Sorcerer. The old man is talking to a broom! There is a flash of lightning and the broom starts to dance across the room. It sweeps up the pieces of glass!

Jim is very happy. He has heard the magic words at last!

The Sorcerer still has not seen Jim in the corner of the Great Hall. Jim gets up very quietly and goes upstairs to bed. It is long after midnight.

Before he goes to sleep Jim says the magic words to himself again and again.

The next morning he gets up very early. He wants to use the magic words. He wants to make a spell.

"Be careful!" the raven says. "Don't let the Sorcerer hear you. Wait till he goes out."

At last the old man leaves the castle. The raven watches him.

"Now you can start," the raven tells Jim.

"Bring the water for the cauldron, broom," Jim says. Then he says the magic words.

At once the broom grows two long thin arms. It picks up two buckets and runs out of the Great Hall. Jim and the raven follow the broom to the river.

The broom works very quickly and soon the cauldron is full. But the broom brings more and more buckets of water.

"Quickly!" the raven shouts. "Stop it! Stop it!"

"I can't stop it!" Jim cries. "I don't know the right magic words. I can start spells but I can't *stop* them!"

The broom brings more and more buckets of water to the Great Hall. Soon there is water all over the floor and it is getting deeper and deeper.

Jim tries to stop the broom. He picks up an axe and chops the broom into two pieces. But – oh, no! Each half of the broom grows arms and now *two* brooms are bringing buckets of water!

Soon the whole castle is full of water.

Then the Sorcerer comes back. His great shadow falls onto Jim and the raven. He is very, very angry. He shouts the magic words and again there is a flash of lightning. The broom stops at once. The Sorcerer uses his magic and soon all the water disappears.

Jim smiles. He has heard the other magic words at last. Now he can stop spells, too.

The Sorcerer is still very angry with Jim.

"Hit him! Hit him!" he tells the broom. There is another flash of lightning, but then Jim shouts his magic words. The broom stops. It goes and stands in the corner of the Great Hall.

Jim is very happy.

"That's the end of you," Jim tells the Sorcerer. "I'm not afraid of you now. I can start spells and I can stop them, too. You've let me hear the other magic words at last!" And he dances round and round the Sorcerer.

But the raven flies away. He goes and sits high up near the ceiling of the Great Hall. He is very frightened.

The Sorcerer smiles at Jim but it is not a friendly smile.

"Come here, boy," he says. Then he goes on quietly, "Of course you've learned my secrets. You're a clever boy. You're my best apprentice."

Jim is surprised. Has the Sorcerer suddenly changed?

"Be careful, Jim," the raven calls. "The Sorcerer is still dangerous."

The raven is right!

Suddenly there is a flash of lightning and the Sorcerer becomes an angry bear! The bear hits Jim and he falls to the floor. Jim tries to escape but he cannot.

The raven flies down from the ceiling.

"Change yourself into a snake!" he cries. "Bears hate snakes!"

Quickly Jim says the magic words and becomes a snake. But the bear changes, too. There is another flash of lightning and the bear becomes an eagle. Again Jim tries to escape but the eagle holds the snake's tail.

"Change again! Change again!" the raven cries.

This time Jim becomes a wildcat. It jumps up at the eagle but the eagle is too quick. It flies away.

The eagle flies out of the castle. The wildcat follows it.

When the eagle arrives at the river it suddenly disappears.

The wildcat looks into the water.

"Where has the Sorcerer gone?" he asks.

A little silver fish puts its head out of the water. "You can't catch me," it says. "You're only an apprentice. My magic will always be greater than yours."

The Sorcerer has become a fish.

"I'll become a boy again," Jim tells the raven. "Then I'll go into the river and catch the fish."

"No, I've got a better idea," the raven replies. And he says something in Jim's ear.

"Listen to me, Sorcerer!" Jim shouts. "If you're so clever, show me!"

"Yes, I will," the Sorcerer answers. "This time I'll become a mountain!"

"Oh, no," Jim replies. "Change yourself into something very small. That's more difficult. Become a drop of water!"

There is a big flash of lightning and then – nothing.

Jim is standing in the water. He can hear only the sound of the river. It runs down the mountain into the valley and then far away into the great sea.

Jim and the raven are very happy. They dance together by the river. They laugh and laugh.

"We've won! We've won!" Jim cries. "The Sorcerer is a drop of water now. Soon he'll be lost in the sea!"

"Yes, the Sorcerer has gone for ever," the raven cries. "We're free at last!"

And the two friends go down the mountain.

The people in the village are very happy to see Jim again.

"What happened at the castle?" they want to know. "You were away

for a long time. We thought that you were dead."

Jim tells them his story again and again.

"You were very brave," the people tell him.

"Can you still do magic?" they ask him.

"Yes, I can," Jim says. "But I'll always use my magic carefully, I promise."

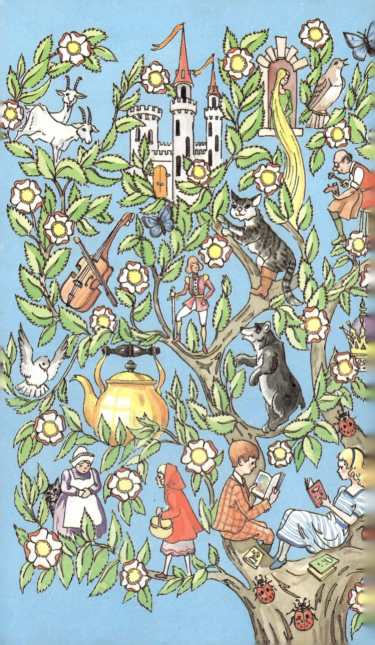